Shakespeare Alive

Shakespeare Today

Jane Shuter

Heinemann
LIBRARY

Chicago, Illinois

Edited by Andrew Farrow and Abby Colich
Designed by Steve Mead
Original illustrations © Capstone Global Library Ltd 2014
Picture research by Elizabeth Alexander
Production by Victoria Fitzgerald
Originated by Capstone Global Library Ltd
Printed and bound in China by Leo Paper Group

17 16 15 14 13
10 9 8 7 6 5 4 3 2 1

Library of Congress Cataloging-in-Publication Data
Shuter, Jane.
  Shakespeare today / Jane Shuter.
    pages cm.—(Shakespeare alive)
  Includes bibliographical references and index.
  ISBN 978-1-4329-9631-4 (hb)—ISBN 978-1-4329-9635-2 (pb)
1. Shakespeare, William, 1564–1616—Influence. 2. Shakespeare, William, 1564–1616—Criticism and interpretation. I. Title.

  PR2976.S49 2014
  822.3'3—dc23   2013018043

Acknowledgments
We would like to thank the following for permission to reproduce photographs: Alamy: pp. 5 (© The Art Archive), 17 (© Moviestore collection Ltd), 19 (© Keystone Pictures USA), 25 (© AF archive), 33 (© Toddlerstock), 36 (© Lebrecht Music and Arts Photo Library), 37 (© Geraint Lewis), 44 (© NiKreative), 47 (© Bernie Epstein), 54 (© Dave G. Houser); Getty Images: pp. 6 (DEA Picture Library), 40 (William Hogarth/The Bridgeman Art Library); Lebrecht Music & Arts: p. 12 (Tristram Kenton); McCurdy & Co: pp. 48, 49; Rex Features: p. 21 (Alastair Muir); Shakespeare's Globe: pp. 8 (photograph by Simon Annand, 2012), 11 (photograph by Ellie Kurttz, 2010), 15 (photograph by Ellie Kurttz, 2010), 23 (photograph by Simon Kane, 2012), 27 (photograph by Simon Kane, 2012), 51 (photograph by Manuel Harlan, 2011), 53 (CGI by Allies and Morrison); St. Mary's University College. Pictured: Matthew Hahn, John Kani, Atandwa Kani - Richmond Theatre, March 2008, reading of 'The Robben Island Bible: p. 43; Superstock: pp. 32 (Universal Images Group), 38 (National Portrait Gallery); TopFoto.co.uk: p. 28 (Richard Campbell / ArenaPAL).

Cover photograph of *Romeo and Juliet* (1996) reproduced with permission of The Kobal Collection (20th Century Fox/Morton, Merrick).

We would like to thank Farah Karim-Cooper for her invaluable help in the preparation of this book.

Every effort has been made to contact copyright holders of material reproduced in this book. Any omissions will be rectified in subsequent printings if notice is given to the publisher.

All the Internet addresses (URLs) given in this book were valid at the time of going to press. However, due to the dynamic nature of the Internet, some addresses may have changed, or sites may have changed or ceased to exist since publication. While the author and publisher regret any inconvenience this may cause readers, no responsibility for any such changes can be accepted by either the author or the publisher.

Contents

Shakespeare Today 4

Did Shakespeare Write Shakespeare? 6

Performing Shakespeare 8

Playing Hamlet.. 20

Using Shakespeare...................................... 22

Ophelia—A Life of Her Own 32

Who Did Shakespeare Use? 34

Macbeth... 36

Always Famous? 38

Reacting to Shakespeare................................ 42

Global Shakespeare 44

Shakespeare Festivals..................................... 54

What's the Story? 56

Famous Performances 58

Glossary.. 61

Find Out More 63

Index.. 64

Some words are shown in bold, **like this**. You can find out what they mean by looking in the glossary.

Shakespeare Today

Shakespeare is world famous. He wrote his plays and poems over 400 years ago, yet he's more widely recognized than any other modern English **playwright**. Nearly 500,000 people visit the Royal Shakespeare Company's (RSC) theaters each year. Many more tourists flock to visit his birthplace, Stratford-upon-Avon, spending money on food, accommodation, and souvenirs, which benefits the local area.

Shakespeare's Influence

Shakespeare's most obvious influence is that large numbers of people go to see his plays performed, not only by **national companies** such as the RSC, but also by small local and student groups. His plays and poems are also studied in schools worldwide. As a result, many people can quote Shakespeare's most famous lines. Some actors feel intimidated by Shakespeare's best-known speeches. They feel that many audience members are saying these speeches to themselves, along with the actors.

This is from a modern graphic novel version of *Macbeth*.

Other Influences

Shakespeare's influence has stretched much further than just the performance of his works. His stories have been adapted by other playwrights, authors, poets, and filmmakers. In 2005, alone there were 16 films made of his plays. However, his influence is much greater than that—especially his influence on the English language. For example, he invented and first used the following everyday words and phrases: *assassination*, *hot-blooded*, and *useful*, among many others.

This famous engraving of Shakespeare was made by Martin Droeshout for the *First Folio* collection of Shakespeare's plays, published in 1623. Its editors knew Shakespeare, so many people think it is most likely to resemble him.

DID YOU KNOW?

Copyright

Most countries today have copyright laws. These laws stop people from copying the creative work of someone in that country, such as a playwright's play, without permission. However, this protection only lasts for a certain time, usually less than one hundred years. Anyone can use Shakespeare's words today without it being illegal. At the time, as a playwright, Shakespeare didn't own the copyright of his plays. He sold each play to an acting **company**. It was then the only group with the right to put on that play, unless they sold it to a publisher to print, which didn't happen very often. Once plays were printed and sold, they could be put on by anyone.

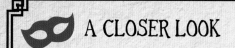
Did Shakespeare Write Shakespeare?

Because Shakespeare lived so long ago, we know little about him. For example, we don't know where he went to school, but we can infer from his family's status that he received a basic education in Stratford.

A portrait from the time that many scholars think is Christopher Marlowe.

William Shakespeare

The following is most of what we know for certain about William Shakespeare. He was born in Stratford-upon-Avon, England, in 1564. His father was a **glover** and was an important man in the town. William probably attended the town **grammar school**. He married Anne Hathaway in 1582, and they had three children. He was first mentioned as a playwright in London in 1592. He died in Stratford-upon-Avon in 1616.

At first, no one doubted that William Shakespeare wrote the plays that were known as his. Then, in 1785, a man named James Wilmot said Shakespeare could not have written the plays. He argued that a young man from a small English town, with only a grammar school education, was not educated or **sophisticated** enough. Wilmot's argument took hold. Some people began to hunt for the "real" Shakespeare. Who did they suggest had written the plays?

Francis Bacon

Wilmot's suggestion was Francis Bacon, a **scholar** and scientist. In Bacon's **favor** were his university education and the fact he was a writer. However, he had no connection to the theater, and even wrote about it as a waste of time. Bacon was known for his **essays** and scientific works, not plays or poetry.

Edward de Vere, Earl of Oxford

In 1920, a schoolteacher named J. T. Looney suggested the Earl of Oxford had written the plays. In the Earl of Oxford's favor were his excellent education and the fact he was a sophisticated **nobleman**. He wrote poetry under his own name, though it was not considered to be as good as Shakespeare's. He also wrote plays, which have not survived. However, if he wrote Shakespeare's plays, why not publish them under his own name? Also, the Earl of Oxford died in 1604, before many of the plays were even written.

Christopher Marlowe

Christopher Marlowe was a playwright at the same time as Shakespeare. Supporting the argument that Marlowe wrote the plays are his age and his writing skills. However, he was killed in a fight in a tavern in 1593, when only a few Shakespeare plays had been written. Those who believe he wrote the plays say he was a government spy who pretended to die to avoid being caught, and Shakespeare agreed to pretend to write plays actually written by Marlowe.

The Rest

Some people have suggested the plays were written by others, including nobles, Queen Elizabeth I, or even several people working together—there are about 50 candidates in all.

William Shakespeare

The case for William Shakespeare from Stratford writing Shakespeare's works is the most convincing. He is known to have **collaborated** with other playwrights, but this was usual at the time. He probably only had a grammar school education, but this is true of other playwrights from the time, including the famous Ben Jonson. The plays have their own patterns of **verse** and use of language. Scholars are confident they were all written by the same person (and his collaborators) and are different from surviving works by other candidates. We don't know exactly how many plays Shakespeare wrote, or the order he wrote them in. However, the evidence is not strong for any candidate. Additionally, other playwrights at the time refer to him as a playwright, and from 1598 several publishers printed plays under his name.

Performing Shakespeare

Today, Shakespeare's plays are performed in many different ways. Some companies like to perform Shakespeare using stages, costumes, and **props** similar to those of his time to give audiences today a feel for what performances were like then. Others want the freedom to interpret Shakespeare's plays in their own way.

Original Practices

At Shakespeare's Globe, a theater in London, England, that is a **reconstruction** of the first Globe theater of Shakespeare's time, some plays have been performed following **original practices**. This means trying to get as close to performances of the time as possible. To do this, they:

- only use props and special effects used at the time
- have a fairly bare stage without complicated **sets**
- have musicians playing arrangements of songs and music from the time on replicas of instruments of the time
- end the performance (even a tragedy) with a "jig" (dance)

Paul Chahidi plays Maria and Colin Hurley plays Sir Toby Belch in the 2012 production of *Twelfth Night* at the Globe.

- wear costumes made only from materials available at the time, to styles and patterns used by **tailors** and shoemakers at the time
- don't use zippers or Velcro as fastenings (making quick changes of costume far more difficult)
- experiment with speaking the verse as they think it was spoken

Acting in Shakespeare's Time

No one published stage-acting **manuals** in Shakespeare's time. However, **oratory** and **rhetoric**, the arts of speaking in public, were taught in grammar schools, from manuals written at the time and from books by ancient Romans on the subject. Most suggested speaking in a clear, "natural" way, making sure to vary speed and **tone**. Plays of the time give clues about how actors, rather than public speakers, should behave. The most famous is in *Hamlet*, where Hamlet tells some traveling actors the best way to perform the play they are going to present that evening.

Moving Around

The way actors move tells you a lot about what the **characters** they are playing are like. Their facial expressions tell you what the characters are feeling. Japanese Noh theater, for example, has a series of set gestures to convey character and emotions. There is no evidence to show that acting companies in Shakespeare's time had standard movements like this. It is more likely that costumes, wigs, and makeup gave the most clues about the character.

Original Practices in Action

Colin Hurley, an actor who has performed in original practices at the Globe, said in an interview in 2012:

> The most noticeable difference, for me, is the costumes. They need breaking in, like a new pair of shoes. A **doublet** is much more rigid than normal clothes. I always feel much chunkier, more solid, in Elizabethan clothes. You make different shapes. You take up more space with your big pants and your sword swinging around behind you.

Focus on Shakespeare

There are many **theater companies** that concentrate on performing Shakespeare. Like the modern Globe in London, they do perform modern plays and plays by **contemporaries** of Shakespeare, but Shakespeare is their focus. The modern Globe stages many productions in costumes that look "Shakespearean" while not strictly following original practices. The Australian Shakespeare Company, Melbourne, began by staging performances with no theater at all called "Shakespeare under the Stars."

These are just a few of the permanent companies that focus on producing Shakespeare worldwide. There are many companies that run regular Shakespeare festivals. Almost every state in the United States has one!

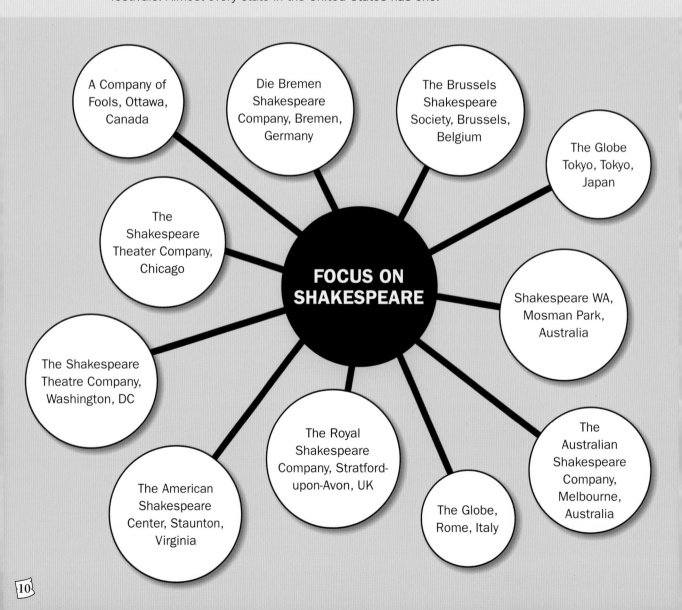

A Company of Fools, Ottawa, Canada

Die Bremen Shakespeare Company, Bremen, Germany

The Brussels Shakespeare Society, Brussels, Belgium

The Globe Tokyo, Tokyo, Japan

The Shakespeare Theater Company, Chicago

FOCUS ON SHAKESPEARE

Shakespeare WA, Mosman Park, Australia

The Shakespeare Theatre Company, Washington, DC

The American Shakespeare Center, Staunton, Virginia

The Royal Shakespeare Company, Stratford-upon-Avon, UK

The Globe, Rome, Italy

The Australian Shakespeare Company, Melbourne, Australia

Directing Shakespeare

Some **directors**, even if they don't use original practices, try to be as true to Shakespeare's plays as possible. They focus on the words and avoid giving the audience their "**take**" on the play. But many directors see it as part of their job to give audiences their own view of a Shakespeare play. For example, they might cut lines, to make the plays shorter and more direct. They might decide to have a young Hamlet, who is still full of teenage angst, or an older Hamlet, a **mature student**, full of indecision. One of the things that make Shakespeare's plays so timeless is that they allow the director to make these types of decisions. There is no descriptive cast list that says, "Hamlet, Prince of Denmark, a 20-year-old student with stoop and a stammer."

BIOGRAPHY

LUCY BAILEY

Director Lucy Bailey studied English at Oxford University from 1981 to 1983. She has directed operas and plays. With Anda Winters, she set up a new 80-seat theater (the Print Room) in 2010. Bailey directed six Shakespeare plays at the Globe and for the RSC between 2006 and 2013: *Titus Andronicus*, *Timon of Athens*, *Macbeth*, *Julius Caesar*, *The Taming of the Shrew*, and *The Winter's Tale*.

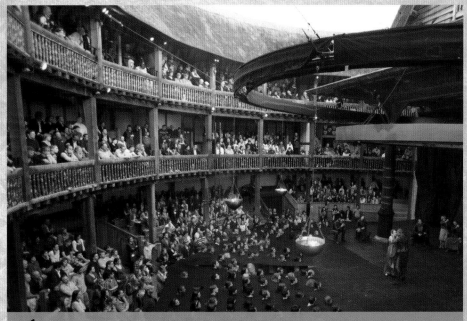

Lucy Bailey's *Macbeth*, at the Globe in 2010, had a black membrane in part of the pit for audience members to put their heads through. It was to make them seem trapped in hell.

Setting the Scene

An important part of a director's view of a Shakespeare play is where and when to set the action. The costumes, stage set, and props are all driven by the director's choice of time and place for the play. Shakespeare made these choices, too. Shakespeare, and other playwrights at the time, often set plays in ancient Greece or Rome, or in imaginary countries.

Sometimes they did this to avoid **censorship**. Every play at the time had to have a **license** to be performed. A government official called the **Master of the Revels** read a play to decide if it had political or religious messages that the government would object to. Sometimes he said parts of a play had to be cut or rewritten before he would give a license. He refused to allow some plays to be performed at all. A Greek or Roman **setting** could help a play get passed. These settings also suited the interest in **classical** ideas at the time. The Greek and Latin languages were both taught in schools.

This photo from the 2005 *Julius Caesar* at the Barbican Theatre in London, shows Caesar (John Shrapnel, in the raincoat) arriving in Rome. The director, Deborah Werner, was making a point about the power of modern politicians in her setting of the play.

DID YOU KNOW?

Politics and Plays

Directors can also use a Shakespeare play to deliver a political message. *Julius Caesar* is a Shakespeare play that tells the story of the assassination of a powerful Roman emperor by people who think he is taking too much power. It is a play that directors often use to get across a political message about power. The time and place that they choose to set the play in can underline their message. In 2012, an all-black production at the RSC was set in modern Africa. The director, Gregory Doran, chose this setting because it reflected political upheavals in that continent, where several countries have been ruled by dictators. He said that Africa also suited the play because of the widespread beliefs in spirits and prophecy that exist there.

Making Choices

Where and when a director chooses to set a play often tells you something about how they have reacted to the story of the play. If they set a play in modern dress, it tells you they think the play has a message that can be applied to life now. A director who sets *A Midsummer Night's Dream* or *Romeo and Juliet* in modern dress may do it to show how the young lovers in the play have feelings and reactions similar to young lovers now. However, at the time Shakespeare was writing, most children had their marriages arranged by their families, as do the lovers in both of these plays. In contrast, a director producing the play now in the United States will need to deal with the fact that there are fewer young people today for whom this is true. The director might choose to ignore this fact, or do something to highlight it.

Not Just Words on a Page

In the 1950s, students could go to college to study English literature without having seen a Shakespeare play performed. They might have written thousands of words analyzing the plays, but never see one. Today, this is very unlikely to happen. This is partly because students have more ways of watching Shakespeare. As well as going to the theater, they can watch a film or DVD, or sometimes watch Shakespeare on TV. It's important that they have these opportunities. Shakespeare's plays were written to be performed, not read. This is when they truly come alive.

Funny Business

People who have never seen a Shakespeare play often complain that the "funny" parts aren't funny. They aren't always funny to read, because the language can be difficult. If you don't know what the words mean, then it's difficult to find it funny. But on stage, with experienced actors, the same words are very funny. The actors will have worked hard to understand the words, and it is their job to get the humor across to the audience.

DID YOU KNOW?

Recognizable People

Shakespeare's plays were written hundreds of years ago, but they work today because they have recognizable people in them. Romeo and Juliet were convincing teenage lovers in the 1600s, and they are convincing teenage lovers now. Juliet's cousin, Tybalt, is recognizable as a young man concerned about being humiliated or not being taken seriously. Romeo's friends, Mercutio and Benvolio, tease him about being in love just as boys tease their friends now. The ideas of conflicting loyalties or romances that families don't approve of are timeless.

This is especially true when a play is performed on a **thrust stage** that sticks out into the audience. The actors can make eye contact with the audience, say their lines as if chatting to the crowd, and even shake hands with audience members or give them things. Interestingly, when watching Shakespeare's plays we can see that even the tragedies have funny scenes in them. The porter in *Macbeth* has very long, complicated speeches. But when the actor plays this character as drunk and rambling, and then teases audience members, it becomes funny.

The porter in *Macbeth*, at the Globe in 2010, had the audience roaring with laughter at speeches that are hard to find funny when read.

Shakespeare on Film

People have been making movies of Shakespeare plays almost since the invention of film. Some have starred famous Shakespearean actors of their time, such as Laurence Olivier (*Henry V*, 1944, *Hamlet*, 1948) and Ian McKellen (*Macbeth* for TV in 1979, *Richard III*, 1995). Others have starred people who were much less likely to perform Shakespeare, or were encouraged to do so by a director. Leonardo DiCaprio played Romeo to Claire Danes' Juliet in *Romeo + Juliet* made in 1996 by director Baz Luhrmann. DiCaprio, who went on to star in *Titanic* in 1997, had been working in TV and films since he was a child, but he had no experience performing in a Shakespeare play. The film cost about $14,500,000 to make and made $11,133,231 on its opening weekend in the United States. It was a huge popular and critical success.

What Makes Film Different?

Cinemas and theaters are very different places. Film and theater directors can both try to make a Shakespeare play relevant to a modern audience, but they can't control who attends. Some people enjoy going to the theater. Those who do not enjoy going may see theater as "too difficult" to appreciate. Also, the average cost of a theater ticket is almost three times that of a movie ticket. In Shakespeare's day, people could stand in the yard of an open-air theater for the price of a loaf of bread. Some theaters have low-priced tickets, but often you have to line up for them on the day of the performance. More people are likely to watch Shakespeare for the first time at the movies, on TV, or via the Internet.

IAN MCKELLEN

Ian McKellen is an actor who has had a lot of experience playing Shakespeare, on stage and on screen. He was born and educated in the United Kingdom and played his first Shakespeare role (Malvolio in *Twelfth Night*) at school. His love of Shakespeare meant he not only performed the plays in theaters all over the world, but he also **toured** a one-man show of speeches from Shakespeare. It is called *Acting Shakespeare*, and he performed it almost every year from 1977 to 1990.

Ian McKellen (on the right) played Richard III in the film *Richard III*, made in 1995.

Unlikely Performers

Some people have appeared in Shakespeare on film and on TV who are famous for a very different type of acting—or even for something other than acting. Mel Gibson, most famous for action films, played Hamlet in a 1990 film of *Hamlet* directed by Franco Zeffirelli. John Cleese, more famous as a member of the *Monty Python's Flying Circus* comedy team, played Petruchio in *The Taming of the Shrew* for the British Broadcasting Corporation (BBC) in 1980. His performance was a huge success, as was the whole production.

DID YOU KNOW?

All 37 plays

Between 1978 and 1985, a BBC project set out to film all 37 Shakespeare plays for TV, in association with Time-Life in the United States. The project had three different producers. One of them, Jonathan Miller, chose several actors who had not played Shakespeare before to take on important roles. John Cleese as Petruchio was the best-known example. Bob Hoskins (who became famous for roles in *Who Framed Roger Rabbit* and *Hook*) played the part of Iago, the villain in *Othello*.

A New Audience

While some performers are nervous about taking on demanding roles in Shakespeare for the first time, many directors like the fact that an unlikely "star" will encourage their fans from their other work to enjoy Shakespeare. Actress Elizabeth Taylor was very nervous about making a movie version of *The Taming of the Shrew* in 1967. However, she turned in a fine performance. Many of her fans watched Shakespeare for the first time—and enjoyed it.

This photo shows the Beatles performing Shakespeare in the *Around the Beatles* British television program in 1964.

Happy 400th Birthday!

On 28 April 1964, a British TV program called *Around the Beatles* celebrated Shakespeare's 400th birthday in an unusual way. The TV studio was given a thrust stage, space for people to stand around it, and two levels of polygonal standing space to roughly imitate an **outdoor theater** from Shakespeare's time. On this stage, the Beatles, a famous musical group who were not actors, performed Shakespeare.

The scene was cleverly chosen. It was the play that the workmen of Athens put on in *A Midsummer Night's Dream*. The whole point of this play-within-a-play is that the workmen are not good actors. This means it didn't matter that the Beatles were not trained actors either.

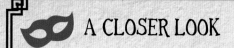

Playing Hamlet

Hamlet is one of Shakespeare's most famous, and widely quoted, plays. It is the play that many directors want to direct, and Hamlet is one of the roles that many actors want to play.

Who Has Played Hamlet?

The list of who has played Hamlet in well-known theaters and films is a long one. Laurence Olivier was in *Hamlet* on stage and film. The film of his *Hamlet*, made in 1948, is the only Shakespeare play to have won an Oscar for best actor and best film. Richard Burton was in the longest-running Broadway production of *Hamlet* in New York, which was also filmed in 1964. David Tennant played Hamlet at the RSC in 2008. Jude Law played Hamlet in London in 2009, and then went on tour with the show in the United States and to Kronborg Castle, at Elsinore in Denmark where *Hamlet* is set.

DID YOU KNOW?

Female Hamlets

Not all of the actors who want to play Hamlet are men. Women have played him, too—both in all-female companies and in mixed ones. Here are a few highlights:

- 1900 – Sarah Bernhardt played Hamlet on stage and screen.
- 1920 – Asta Nielsen starred as Hamlet in a silent film. She played Hamlet as a woman who had to disguise herself as a man.
- 2000 – Angela Winkler played Hamlet in Germany and at the Edinburgh Festival in Scotland.
- 2012 – Alix Cuadra played Hamlet in all-female production of Hamlet in San Francisco, California.

DID YOU KNOW?

Tchaikowsky's Skull

Mr. André Tchaikowsky left most of his body to science when he died in 1982. However, he left his skull to the RSC, asking that it be used in a performance. Mr. Tchaikowsky's skull was used in the 2008 production of *Hamlet* and, later, in the RSC film of the play, released on DVD in 2010. In 2011, a set of stamps celebrated the 50th anniversary of the RSC. David Tennant, as Hamlet, is shown holding Mr. Tchaikowsky's skull on one of the stamps.

Here is David Tennant as Hamlet, in 2008. The skull is that of Mr. André Tchaikowsky, a famous Polish pianist and composer who died in 1982.

Using Shakespeare

Some writers and directors have made **adaptations** of Shakespeare's plays and updated the original language. Some of these adaptations are more obvious than others. For example, the title of the 1955 film, *Joe Macbeth*, was a fairly heavy hint that it was a reworking of Shakespeare's *Macbeth*! British director Ken Hughes set the film in the world of American gangsters, having Joe Macbeth "**rub out**" gang leader Duce and take over his empire.

Joe Macbeth—Again

In 2005, the BBC made a series called "ShakespeaRe-told." It told the stories of *Macbeth*, *A Midsummer Night's Dream*, *The Taming of the Shrew*, and *Much Ado About Nothing* as if they were modern dramas. *Macbeth* was about a chef called Joe Macbeth who murders to become a TV celebrity chef.

DID YOU KNOW?

Sci-Fi Shakespeare

At least one Shakespeare story has been reworked by setting it in outer space. *Forbidden Planet* was a film made in 1956, loosely based on Shakespeare's *The Tempest*. It cost almost $2 million to make, the most anyone had spent on a science fiction film at that time. It became a cult classic. In the 1980s, a musical based on it, *Return to the Forbidden Planet*, became popular. The musical won Britain's Olivier Award for Best New Musical in 1990. It is now regularly performed by **amateur** and professional companies.

At the London Globe to Globe Festival in 2012, the Q Brothers from Chicago, Illinois, played a hip-hop version of *Othello* where Othello is a famous DJ. They have also turned *The Comedy of Errors* and *Much Ado About Nothing* into hip-hop performances.

Snappy Shakespeare

The Reduced Shakespeare Company, established in 1981, became famous for its fast and furious run through all the plots of Shakespeare's plays in one show with four actors. The performance began with *Hamlet* in 20 minutes and added plays until, in 1987, the company played *The Complete Works of William Shakespeare* (abridged) in one hour. The plays had a variety of styles. *Othello* was rap and *Titus Andronicus* was performed as a TV cooking show. Today, The Reduced Shakespeare Company has several companies touring worldwide and playing to packed theaters.

Musical Shakespeare

In 1692, English composer Henry Purcell produced a version of *A Midsummer Night's Dream* with sections of his own music. Many people see this as the first Shakespeare musical. It has been followed by many musicals, famous and not-so-famous. *West Side Story* is a well-known musical based on *Romeo and Juliet*, but other musicals have been based on the story, including a rock musical (1999) and two French versions (2001 and 2004).

Operatic Shakespeare

There have also been many operas of Shakespeare's stories, from the German *Romeo und Julie* (1776) to Thomas Adès' *Tempest* (2004). Giuseppe Verdi wrote three famous operas based on Shakespeare's stories: *Macbeth* (1847), *Otello* (1887), and *Falstaff* (based on *The Merry Wives of Windsor*, 1893).

DID YOU KNOW?

Shakespeare and Street Gangs

West Side Story was a 1957 musical based on the story of *Romeo and Juliet*. It took Jerome Robbins about ten years to get **funding** for this version about two rival street gangs in New York City, using modern **dialogue**. Leonard Bernstein, who wrote the music, said that the show "couldn't depend on stars, being about kids." Without stars as an attraction, it was difficult to finance the show. But once it was launched, it was hugely popular. In 1961, it was made into a film which won 10 Oscars. This musical has been translated into 26 languages and played regularly by professional and amateur companies all around the world.

Shakespeare and Young People

Shakespeare's stories have been retold for students in a variety of ways with the aim of getting young people interested in Shakespeare. For example, manga retellings of Shakespeare keep the titles of the plays, but use manga-style cartoons to give a very cut down version of the stories. Other retellings use Shakespeare's own lines, but cut out many lines to offer a shorter version of a play. Some turn the plays into modern language. Films such as *10 Things I Hate About You* (a reworking of *The Taming of the Shrew*) have set Shakespeare's stories in schools or in teenage gangs.

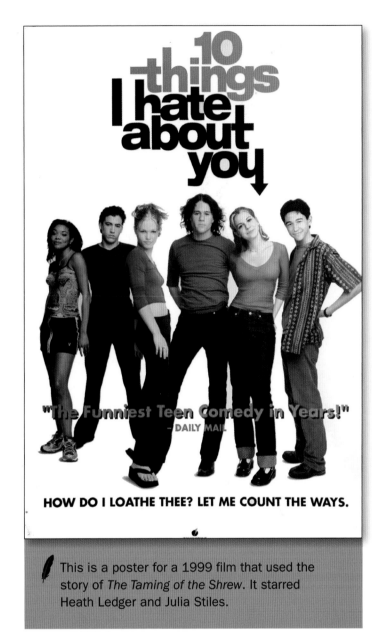

This is a poster for a 1999 film that used the story of *The Taming of the Shrew*. It starred Heath Ledger and Julia Stiles.

Stealthy Shakespeare

Some retellings of Shakespeare's stories are hard to recognize at first. *The Lion King*, a 1994 Disney cartoon in which the "prince" whose father is murdered is a lion cub named Simba, was partly based on *Hamlet*. The cartoon has been made into a popular musical that has toured the world. The producer said that the story was **pitched** to her as "Bambi in Africa meets *Hamlet*."

Translating Shakespeare's Plays

Shakespeare has been translated into hundreds of languages, from Arabic to Zulu. Translation means changing the language, but some translators try to keep to poetic **formal** language, close to Shakespeare's words. They try to convey the feel of Shakespeare, as well as the story. Other translators produce plays that are very modern in language and just tell the same story. Shakespeare's works have also been translated into sign language. He has even been quoted on the TV program *Star Trek*—in the Klingon language!

DID YOU KNOW?

Inspiring Japanese films

Akira Kurosawa, a famous Japanese filmmaker, based the plots of several of his most famous films on Shakespeare plays, changing them to reflect Japanese culture. *Throne of Blood* (1957) is based on *Macbeth* and *Ran* (1985) is based on *King Lear*. He also adapted Japanese and Russian stories—over half of his films were based on the works of others. In turn, his work influenced many other film-makers' works, including George Lucas' *Star Wars* and John Sturges' *The Magnificent Seven*.

Cultural Differences

Translators of Shakespeare have to tackle the language and also deal with the beliefs and **culture** of Shakespeare's time. The culture of other countries can have a big impact on their understanding of a play. People might even react more like an audience from Shakespeare's time than a modern audience. For example, in *A Midsummer Night's Dream*, Egeus is angry with his daughter, Hermia, because she doesn't want to marry the man Egeus has chosen. She wants to marry someone else. The Duke of Athens tells Hermia the laws of Athens say she must marry her father's choice, become a nun, or be killed. Audiences in communities where arranged marriages are the norm, as they were in Shakespeare's time, are likely to react to the problem as Shakespeare's audiences did.

This photo is from the Japanese version of *Titus Andronicus*, from the 2012 Globe to Globe season at the Globe theater in London.

Audiences where arranged marriages are less usual may react differently. Different plays are more popular in different countries. *Hamlet* is the most popular play in the Arab world and in Denmark.

Foreign Films

Shakespeare's stories have also been used by foreign filmmakers. *Hamlet* has been produced in many languages, from the French silent version of 1907 to the Chinese version of 2006. One very popular version was the 1964 Russian *Hamlet* (*Gamlet*, directed by Grigori Kozintsev), which won several European film awards.

A Step Further

Some people have created works that are related to Shakespeare plays, but take them a step further. *Dunsinane*, a play written by David Greig, picks up the story of *Macbeth* where that play ended. Greig asked himself, "What happened after Macbeth was killed and the English defeated his army?" He then wrote *Dunsinane* in 2010 for the RSC as part of their commitment to produce plays as well as performing Shakespeare. Several of these new plays have had connections to Shakespeare. For example, *The Herbal Bed* (1996) is a play about Shakespeare's daughter, Susanna, taking a neighbor to court for slandering her. It is based on a court case that actually happened. *Jubilee* (2001) is about the first festival at Stratford to celebrate the birth of Shakespeare. It was organized in 1769 by the famous English actor David Garrick.

This photo is from the RSC production of *Dunsinane* in 2010.

"Improving" the Plays

Several people have tried to "improve" Shakespeare's plays. Thomas Bowdler produced an edition of the plays in 1807 called *The Family Shakespeare*. All parts of the plays that he thought were "unsuitable" for women and children were cut out. Bowdler's edition completely left out 14 of Shakespeare's plays. Some people liked it because, apart from the cuts, it didn't change the words. However, many people laughed at the idea, and by 1838 a new term had entered the English language: "to bowdlerize." This means "to omit or alter words or passages of a work that are considered **indelicate**, or rude."

Bowdler's Explanation

Thomas Bowdler offered the following explanation of why he created *The Family Shakespeare*:

"I acknowledge Shakespeare to be the world's greatest dramatic poet, but regret that no parent could place the uncorrected book in the hands of his daughter, and therefore I have prepared *The Family Shakespeare*.... Many words and expressions occur which are of so indecent a nature as to make it highly desirable that they should be erased."

Happy Endings

In Shakespeare's time, one thing clearly distinguished a comedy from a tragedy, no matter how much disaster a comedy had, or how much humor a tragedy had. Comedies ended happily and tragedies did not. But some people felt the need to "save" characters they became attached to. One of the most frequently amended plays is *King Lear*. The first time this was done was a version by Nahum Tate in 1681 where Lear lives and regains his throne, and Cordelia lives and marries Edgar. *Romeo and Juliet* was also changed to create a happy ending starting with David Garrick's 1748 adaptation and an opera version by Georg Benda in 1776. In both cases the lovers survive.

Making Poetry

Most of Shakespeare's poetry, and much of the verse in his plays, are written in iambic pentameter. In this type of writing, there are ten syllables in each line, split into five pairs. The second syllable of each pair is stressed. For example, "Shall **I** com**PARE** thee **TO** a **SUM**mer's **DAY**?" Shakespeare was not the first to use iambic pentameter, but he uses it very creatively. The ordinary people in his plays don't speak in verse, but in conversational **prose**. Shakespeare uses unrhymed iambic pentameter much of the time, but uses rhyme for the most poetic or stirring speeches.

Inspiring Poetry

Shakespeare has inspired many poets. In 1619, when the famous English actor Richard Burbage died, an anonymous person wrote an elegy, or death poem, about his life. It lists all his great roles—all from Shakespeare plays. Since then John Keats, Ted Hughes, Sylvia Plath, and James Richardson have all produced Shakespeare-inspired poetry.

DID YOU KNOW?

Creative Spelling

The English language was expanding in Shakespeare's time, but spelling was still very flexible. Shakespeare was famous for spelling his names in many different ways, which was common at the time. Words were spelled in many different ways, too. Some people suggest that the various spellings reflect the speech accents of the people writing the words. However, the same person often spelled the same word in several different ways, which they often do. Even when people tried to establish spelling rules, they often did a poor job. In 1604, a dictionary called *A Table Alphabeticall of Hard Words* spelled "words" in two different ways on the title page!

Shakespeare and Language

Shakespeare lived at a time when the English language was expanding rapidly. Playwrights were especially inventive with words, perhaps because of the demands of the verse style they wrote in. They even made up new words or turned existing words into different parts of speech. For example, Shakespeare took the noun *assassin* and invented the word *assassination*. Between 1500 and 1650, about 12,000 new English words were used for the first time. Shakespeare coined new words from the very beginning of his career as a playwright. About 2,035 words have their first recorded use in a work by Shakespeare. *Hamlet* has 600 new words, such as *survivor* and *unpolluted*.

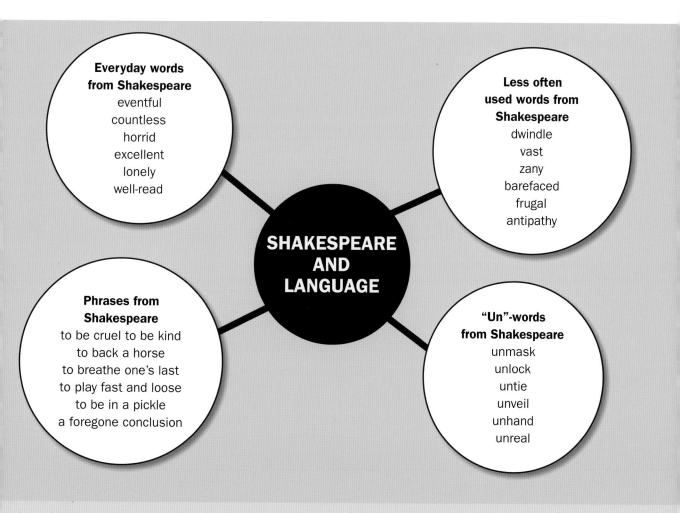

Everyday words from Shakespeare
eventful
countless
horrid
excellent
lonely
well-read

Less often used words from Shakespeare
dwindle
vast
zany
barefaced
frugal
antipathy

SHAKESPEARE AND LANGUAGE

Phrases from Shakespeare
to be cruel to be kind
to back a horse
to breathe one's last
to play fast and loose
to be in a pickle
a foregone conclusion

"Un"-words from Shakespeare
unmask
unlock
untie
unveil
unhand
unreal

Here are just a few examples of words and phrases first written by William Shakespeare that are used in our language today.

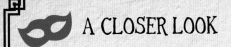
Ophelia—A Life of Her Own

Shakespeare's characters have often inspired people to produce famous works of art and literature. In *Hamlet*, the character of Ophelia is rejected by Hamlet and goes mad when her father is accidentally murdered by Hamlet. Then we are told she has drowned. The Pre-Raphaelite painter John Everett Millais created a painting called *Ophelia* in 1851 and 1852. His painting instantly became popular and remains so to this day. Millais painted several copies, in both watercolors and oils. The painting is so famous that many other artists have "borrowed" it or referred to it in their own art.

One of Millais' oil paintings of *Ophelia*. He painted the landscape outdoors, in Surrey, England. He painted the figure of Ophelia in his studio.

DID YOU KNOW?

The model who posed for Milais' "Ophelia" was Elizabeth Siddal, a popular model of the time. She had to pose lying in a bath in Millais' studio regularly for four months. The water in the bath was kept warm by lamps underneath it. Once, the lamps went out and she caught a bad cold. Her father threatened to sue Millais, who eventually paid the doctor's bills for Elizabeth's treatment.

Millais' *Ophelia* Many Different Ways

Many painters have imitated Millais' famous painting. But it has also been used by artists who use other media to create their work, such as sculpture, collage, or photography. It has also been used by people creating advertisements or other common images.

This shows a Barbie doll as Ophelia, by photographer Neil Juggins. It was taken in 2007.

Who Did Shakespeare Use?

So far we have looked at Shakespeare's influence and how people have used his work. However, Shakespeare also borrowed both plots and characters for his plays. At the time, most writers did this. Their story didn't have to be new, but they did have to tell it well, or with a new twist, for it to become popular. Playwrights at the time were helped by the fact that more and more books, pamphlets, and plays were being printed and sold quite cheaply. There were even translations of foreign books and plays.

Shakespeare used stories from Raphael Holinshed's *Chronicles of England, Scotland and Ireland*, first published in 1577, as a source for *Macbeth* and for all his history plays. He borrowed the plots of earlier plays (in English and in other languages) and also stories told by Greek and Roman authors. As well as stories, Shakespeare borrowed language, chunks of text, and **imagery** from the same sources as the plots.

DID YOU KNOW?

Borrowing Lines

Playwrights in Shakespeare's time didn't just borrow plots. Memorable lines were borrowed, too. In *Romeo and Juliet*, Shakespeare reworked some lines from Christopher Marlowe's play *The Jew of Malta*. The lines are now famous as Shakespeare's. In Marlowe's play, the lines are "But stay! What star shines yonder in the East?/The lodestone of my life, if Abigail." In *Romeo and Juliet*, the lines are "But soft, what light in yonder window breaks? It is the east, and Juliet the sun!" He reworks several more lines from Marlowe throughout the play and lifts one line directly: "Whoever loved that loved not at first sight?"

Added Magic

The important thing for audiences then and now is not that Shakespeare borrowed the plots of stories, but what he did with them and how he made the characters come alive. For example, a simple short story can be turned into a great play by writing good dialogue that makes the characters more realistic and complicated. Shakespeare also tweaked the stories he borrowed to make them more powerful. He based *King Lear* on another play called *King Leir*, which had a happy ending! Shakespeare's tragic ending is far more powerful.

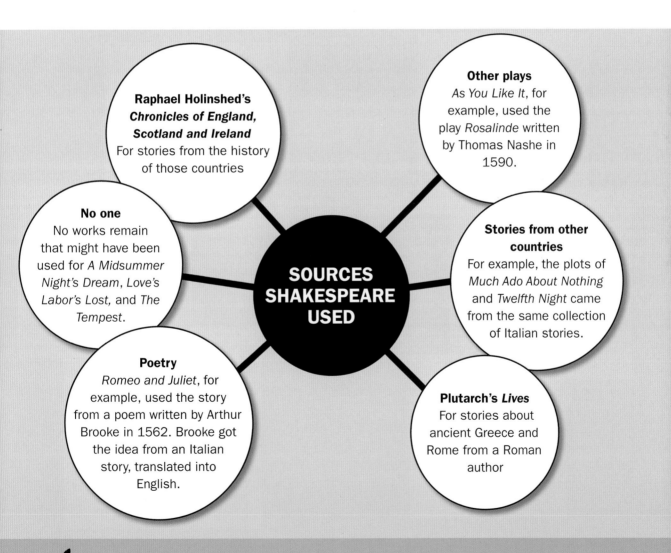

Other plays
As You Like It, for example, used the play *Rosalinde* written by Thomas Nashe in 1590.

Raphael Holinshed's ***Chronicles of England, Scotland and Ireland***
For stories from the history of those countries

No one
No works remain that might have been used for *A Midsummer Night's Dream, Love's Labor's Lost,* and *The Tempest.*

SOURCES SHAKESPEARE USED

Stories from other countries
For example, the plots of *Much Ado About Nothing* and *Twelfth Night* came from the same collection of Italian stories.

Poetry
Romeo and Juliet, for example, used the story from a poem written by Arthur Brooke in 1562. Brooke got the idea from an Italian story, translated into English.

Plutarch's ***Lives***
For stories about ancient Greece and Rome from a Roman author

Here are some examples the kinds of sources Shakespeare used.

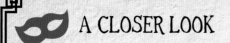

Macbeth

Let's take a closer look at what influenced Shakespeare when he wrote *Macbeth* and how the play has influenced others. Shakespeare's main source was Holinshed's book *Chronicles of England, Scotland and Ireland* published in 1577. Some of the imagery in *Macbeth* comes from tragedies written by the Roman playwright Seneca. Shakespeare was also influenced by the preferences of England's new king. *Macbeth* was written in about 1606, not long after Queen Elizabeth I died and James VI of Scotland became James I of England in 1603. Shortly after James became king he made himself patron of Shakespeare's company and it was renamed the King's Men.

This engraving of Macbeth and Banquo meeting the witches is from Holinshed's *Chronicles of England, Scotland and Ireland*.

PATRICK STEWART

Patrick Stewart was born and educated in the United Kingdom. He left school early and got a job to earn money to go to drama school. After drama school, he worked in various theaters, joining the RSC for the first time in 1966. In 1987, Stewart went to Los Angeles, California, to play Captain Picard in *Star Trek: The Next Generation*. He has worked in the theater and film ever since, including playing Macbeth in the United Kingdom in 2007. The play was such a success that it was made into a movie. This has happened to a few other very successful plays, including Ian McKellen's *Richard III*, but not many.

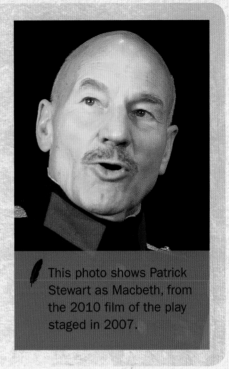

This photo shows Patrick Stewart as Macbeth, from the 2010 film of the play staged in 2007.

King James I

How might Shakespeare have had King James I in mind when he wrote *Macbeth*? The play was set in Scotland and was about who should rule the country. James' family, the Stuarts, claimed their right to rule Scotland all the way back to the time of the character Banquo, who the play shows as someone whose descendants would rule Scotland. Banquo is also shown as a sympathetic character, which would please King James. Witchcraft was a hot topic at the time *Macbeth* was written. In 1597, King James had written a book called *Of Demonology*, which debated whether witches existed and how to identify them. Macbeth's witches show most of the signs given in King James' book.

Influenced by Macbeth

The story of *Macbeth* has been used in films and modern dramas (see pages 22 and 27). Novelists such as Joseph Conrad and William Faulkner have been influenced by the ideas about good and evil in the play. Some novelists have written using other characters from the play, as in *Lady Macbeth* by Susan King. In 1943, the author James Thurber wrote a short story that involved treating the plot of Macbeth as a murder mystery.

Always Famous?

Shakespeare wasn't always as famous as he is now. He was one of many popular playwrights. In many ways, it was the actors, not the plays, which pulled in big audiences. In Shakespeare's time, Richard Burbage was one of the most famous actors. Many of the plays he starred in were written by Shakespeare, but Burbage was more famous.

One of the most famous actresses during Britain's Restoration period was Nell Gwyn, who became the mistress of King Charles II.

Theaters Closed

In 1642, Britain was moving towards **civil war**. Parliament, the government of the nation, closed the theaters. It didn't want crowds to gather because a crowd could turn into an unruly mob. Also, most members of Parliament were **Puritans**. Puritans opposed the theater because they believed it encouraged bad behavior and kept people from going to church. In 1649, King Charles I was executed, and Parliament ruled alone. The theaters remained closed. In 1660, King Charles' son began his rule as Charles II. During this time, known as the Restoration, the theaters were opened. There were many changes in theater. Women were allowed to act on stage. The most important change was that the open-air theaters, such as the Globe, were not reopened or rebuilt. All permanent theaters were **indoor theaters.**

Restoration Love of the New and Modern

After the Restoration, Shakespeare was regularly performed. However, lines were often cut and endings were changed or new material was added. William Davenant's version of *The Tempest* had almost twice as many characters, including newly created sisters for several characters. This was done to create roles for female actresses. People liked the idea of new, modern material. *Macbeth* was hugely popular, but Shakespeare's name seldom appeared on the playbills advertising the performances. Instead, these playbills spoke of "new music," "new songs," or "exciting stage effects."

DID YOU KNOW?

Famous Performers, Not Famous Playwrights

Between 1710 and 1711, ten Shakespeare plays were performed in London with few changes, but only one had publicity material that used his name. Good actors and actresses attracted people to the theater. In the 1740s, a new actor named David Garrick appeared. He was first noticed when he took the part of Richard III in 1741. Onstage, Garrick used an acting style that was more natural than the style used by most actors. He "became" the character he was portraying, rather than striking dramatic poses and saying his lines stiffly, like most actors of the time. Garrick became rich and famous.

Growing Importance

From 1800 onward, Shakespeare became more and more important. People focused on finding, and producing, versions of the plays that were closest to the originals. Shakespeare's poetry also became very popular. His **sonnets**, unlike his plays, were meant to be read. He was talked about as "the greatest playwright of his time," and Shakespeare scholars tried to find out more about him and his life. As the **British Empire** expanded, schools all over the world taught Shakespeare. Also, as English became widely spoken, Shakespeare was studied globally.

BIOGRAPHY

DAVID GARRICK

David Garrick was an 18th-century actor, playwright, and theater manager. He began his acting career in 1741. When he took the lead role in *Richard III*, he was so widely praised that he became a full-time actor. He played 18 different parts in his first 6 months of acting. Garrick was passionate about Shakespeare, and in 1769 launched the first Shakespeare Festival in Stratford. It was supposed to celebrate Shakespeare's 200th birthday, but was about five years late. The celebrations did not include any of Shakespeare's plays, and the festival was abandoned when the Avon River flooded. But the celebrations, and Garrick, brought Shakespeare greater fame. This increased with the printing of inexpensive editions of the plays.

This portrait of David Garrick playing Richard III was painted by the famous artist William Hogarth.

DID YOU KNOW?

A Shakespeare Worshipper
David Garrick built a Greek-style "Temple to Shakespeare" on the grounds of his house in London. In it, he kept a statue of Shakespeare made for him by a French sculptor and various objects supposed to have belonged to Shakespeare, including a glove and a ring. It also contained copies of the plays and a chair said to be made from a tree that once grew in Shakespeare's garden.

Worldwide Importance

Today, Shakespeare is world famous. Every year, thousands of tourists from other countries go to Shakespeare's Globe in London to see a theater similar to the ones where his plays were originally performed. Some of these visitors go to a play, even if they understand very little English. Shakespeare festivals all over the world also draw big audiences. Part of this is because fame has made Shakespeare and his words familiar to people. Many of those who go to see his famous plays have a rough idea of the stories before they go.

DID YOU KNOW?

Bardolatry!
In 1901, the playwright George Bernard Shaw invented a new word for the way people were reacting to Shakespeare: "bardolatry". The word *bard* means "poet" and some people called Shakespeare "the Bard of Avon." The *-olatry* part comes from the word *idolatry*, meaning to worship someone or something almost as a god.

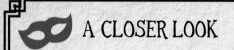

Reacting to Shakespeare

Shakespeare can produce very strong emotions. Some people will tell you that they "hate" Shakespeare, usually because of the way they were taught his works at school. Others will tell you how much they "love" Shakespeare, since they saw a particular performance of one of his plays that really affected them. Here are two examples of how people have reacted to Shakespeare.

Causing a Riot

In 1849, William Macready, a famous English actor, toured the United States with a production of *Macbeth*. On May 10, he performed at the Astor Place Opera House in New York. Wealthy Americans praised his acting style. Many working-class people preferred the more exaggerated acting style of American actor Edwin Forrest. Macready and Forrest had already insulted each other's acting style. Now Forrest announced he would perform *Macbeth* in New York City, on the same day as Macready.

Some supporters of Forrest bought tickets for Macready's *Macbeth*, went into the theater, and began shouting to distract Macready. Outside the theater, thousands of Forrest's supporters were also yelling. Macready supporters began to protest and fighting broke out. The mayor sent in armed troops to stop the riot. They couldn't! Some even had their guns taken by the crowd. Now the crowd was armed. The officer in charge ordered the rioters to break up or the troops would fire. The fighting continued, so the troops opened fire. Twenty-two people were killed and hundreds were injured in the riot.

A Great Consolation

Sonny Venkatrathnam was a political prisoner in Robben Island, South Africa from 1972 to 1978. Another politcal prisoner being held there was Nelson Mandela, who later became president of South Africa (1994–1999). As the political system changed in South Africa, the political prisoners held on Robben Island were released. The last ones left in 1991.

During a time when prisoners were allowed only one book, Venkatrathnam asked for the complete works of Shakespeare. He lent it to other political prisoners and asked them to mark their favorite speech and to date and sign the book. They called it their bible. Inspired by them, Matthew Hahn wrote the play *The Robben Island Bible*. It was based on the speeches that were chosen and interviews with some of the people who chose them. The reactions to readings of the play on Robben Island in 2008, at London's Richmond Theatre in 2009 and at the London's Southbank Centre in 2012 helped shape the final play.

This quote is from *Julius Caesar* (Act 2, Scene 2, spoken by Caesar). It was the speech chosen by Nelson Mandela and signed in *The Robben Island Bible*.

Cowards die many times before their deaths,
The valiant never taste of death but once.
Of all the wonders that I yet have heard,
It seems to me most strange that men should fear,
Seeing that death, a necessary end,
Will come when it will come.

Global Shakespeare

Shakespeare is now the focus of many acting companies, all over the world. Some of these have permanent theaters as company homes. These theaters often have "Shakespeare" in their name, to underline their focus. Some, like the Australian Shakespeare Company (Melbourne, Australia) or the Bremer Shakespeare Company (Bremen, Germany) perform in conventional theaters, or even outdoors. Others perform in theaters that have re-created some of the features of theaters used in Shakespeare's time.

DID YOU KNOW?

Shakespeare in Texas
Richard Garriott of Austin, Texas, has his own replica Elizabethan theater called the Curtain Theater. It was built in 2005 and can seat 350 people. He was inspired to build it by a visit to Shakespeare's Globe in London, and it is home to a permanent company of actors, the Baron's Men. This company only performs Shakespeare, but has both male and female actors.

This photo shows the outside of the Old Globe in Balboa Park, San Diego, California. This representation of London's Globe theater is round and open to the sky. The entire audience sits, and there is no yard to stand in, as there is at the Globe.

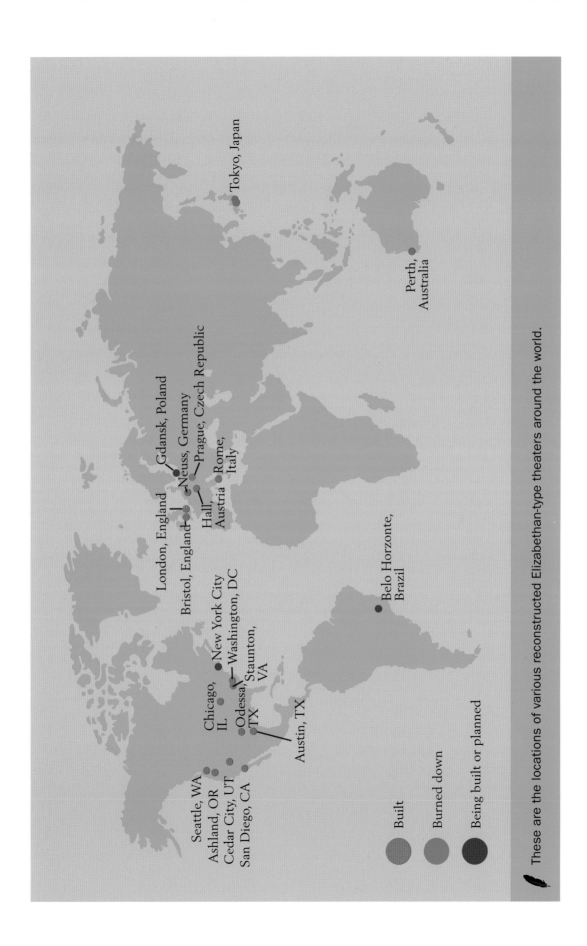

These are the locations of various reconstructed Elizabethan-type theaters around the world.

Why Reconstruct a Theater?

Some "Shakespeare" companies focus entirely on the words; others want to re-create the total experience of acting and attending a play, as well. Many Shakespeare festivals have to settle for an outdoor stage, but some companies want a more permanent structure. They might decide to build a reconstruction of a theater from Shakespeare's time. If they do this, they have several options to choose from. In Shakespeare's time, there were outdoor theaters and indoor theaters, each with advantages and disadvantages for reconstruction.

Outdoor and Indoor Theaters

Outdoor theaters are what people today think of as "Shakespearian" theaters. This type of theater has a large courtyard. The theater is open to the sky and has a "thrust" stage sticking out into it. There is covered seating on three levels, called galleries, all around the yard.

Indoor theaters were smaller and usually built inside another building. The audience sat all the way around a space in the middle, where the actors performed, either in the whole space or on a stage at one end.

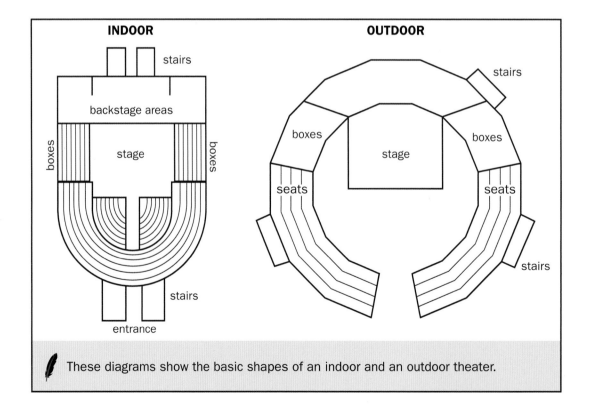

These diagrams show the basic shapes of an indoor and an outdoor theater.

When the RSC built their Swan Theatre in Stratford, they decided to have a thrust stage with galleries around, in the shape of an outdoor theater. However, they didn't want to reproduce an outdoor theater. They put audience comfort and the need for year-round performances first by building a roof and putting seating in the courtyard. The theater opened in 1986.

Indoor theaters have the advantage of being roofed, so they are warm and dry. Outdoor theaters are more recognizably "Shakespearean," so most people base their reconstructions on them. But how far should they go? Do they leave the theater open to the sky? Do they make people stand in the yard, or put seating in? Do they let people call out and interact with the performance, as they did in Shakespeare's time? Do they make the theater look "Shakespearean" on the outside, or just on the inside? The answers depend on what they think audiences will want and the cost of the project.

The Tokyo Globe was opened in 1988. This quote, part of an article in the *New York Times*, shows how most people building replica theaters used the original Globe as a starting point, but not as a blueprint. Unlike the original, the Tokyo Globe has a roof and seating in the yard.

The architect was Arata Isozaki and the Japanese Shakespeare scholars who advised him drew upon three historical sources. To these Mr. Isozaki applied his imagination and his own interest in the neo-classical principles of much Renaissance architecture.

Shakespeare's Globe, London

In 1970, Sam Wanamaker, an American actor and director, set up The Shakespeare Globe Trust in order to build a replica of the original Globe theater of 1599 on the south bank of the Thames River in London. Wanamaker found an architect and builder who were prepared to work, as far as possible, using the building practices of Shakespeare's time. There isn't a lot of evidence about exactly what theaters looked like at the time. There are drawings and writings from the time that can be used, as well as some archaeological evidence. However, a lot of this information is vague, and some of it is conflicting. When the reconstructed Globe was finished in 1996, it was the closest it was possible to get to an exact reproduction of the 1599 Globe.

Building

The builders, McCurdy and Company, used the same techniques and tools carpenters used in Shakespeare's time. However, not everything could be done in the same way. Health and safety regulations meant the builders had to use modern scaffolding and cranes. But every joint was made in the traditional way and the timbers were fixed together using wooden pegs.

Here is builder Peter McCurdy choosing a tree that is now one of the stage pillars at Shakespeare's Globe.

DID YOU KNOW?

First New Thatch Since 1666

Shakespeare's Globe is the first wood and thatch building to be built in London since the Great Fire of London in 1666. Thatch is straw used as a roofing material. The fire caused a huge amount of damage and spread rapidly because houses were timber-framed and thatched. After the fire, a new law declared that all houses built in London had to be made of brick or stone. This doesn't mean they tore down the surviving old timber-framed houses—some still exist today. The regulation applied to new building. McCurdy and Company had to convince the building inspectors that the building would be safe— including trying to set fire to the walls!

The wooden **frame** of the theater was made in "flatpack" frame sections at the workshop and then put together on site, which is also how the original Globe would have been constructed.

Getting Ready for an Audience

The Globe Trust wanted to give modern audiences an experience close to that of an audience in Shakespeare's time. They wanted people standing in the yard and sitting in the galleries. However, they had to consider a modern audience's sense of personal space and comfort. The Trust numbered the bench seats and allowed more space per person than there would have been in Shakespeare's time. They also set a limit of 700 "groundlings"—the people who stood in the yard—in the theater. The theater can hold about 1,500 people. This is perhaps half the number a theater of the same size could hold in Shakespeare's time.

DID YOU KNOW?

Modern Safety

Modern safety regulations mean the modern Globe has more exits than the original one. The thatch has fire-retardant material in it and there are emergency exit signs at various points. The stair towers are larger than they would have been in Shakespeare's time. There also has to be a certain number of staff members and one firefighter on duty for each performance, mainly to help evacuate in case of fire.

Making the Audience Comfortable

The only seating in almost all of the theater is hard wooden benches, except for four "gentleman's rooms" with upright chairs. People can rent cushions to sit on, just as they could in Shakespeare's time. They can also rent blankets in cold weather! There is an intermission, unlike Shakespeare's time, so audiences can walk around, and the groundlings can sit for a while. The audience can also buy snacks and drinks, as they could in Shakespeare's time.

A Great Success

Although it was not quite finished, Shakespeare's Globe opened to the public in 1996 with several performances of *Two Gentlemen of Verona*. It was officially opened the next year. Many people could not imagine that audiences would be willing to sit on hard benches only partly sheltered from the weather for about three hours—let alone stand for almost all that time! But they did. It became hugely popular. By 2012, most Shakespeare performances were sold out all through the season, which runs from April to October.

Who Goes to the Globe?

Many tourists visit Shakespeare's Globe, as do a lot of school groups. They brave the wind and rain, since the actors just keep going no matter what the weather is. There are also many "regulars" from the United Kingdom who go to see every production, every season.

Because the actors and audience can see each other, the audience gets involved in every performance at the Globe. In this photo, Eve Best, in the 2011 *Much Ado About Nothing*, is interacting with the audience, close enough to touch them.

Setting a Trend

The popularity of Shakespeare's Globe meant that other groups were more willing to take the risk of building reproduction theaters. One was built in Prague, Czech Republic, in 1999, modeled on the Globe. Unfortunately, it burned down in 2005. In the same year as the Prague Globe was built, another reproduction theater was built, in Chicago, based on the RSC Swan Theatre in Stratford-upon-Avon. In 2001, the Blackfriars Playhouse, a re-creation of an indoor theater, opened in Virginia. It seats 300, about half the number of the Blackfriars Theatre in London that it is based on.

From a 1999 interview with Karel Klima, director of the Prague Exhibition Grounds where the Prague Globe was built:

"In the first stage, we invested about 10 million crowns ($500,000) into the project. We expect the second stage to cost about another 3 million ($150,000). Then we shall have to decide whether to build a roof or whether to leave it as it is."

On the Drawing Board

More production theaters are being built. McCurdy and Company is helping to plan a Globe for Belo Horizonte, Brazil. Gdansk, Poland, is planning a theater based on one from Gdansk in 1611. It is the only European open-air theater we know of from that time. English actors acted there yearly until 1650. The American Shakespeare Centre in Staunton, Virginia, plans a Globe theater close to their Blackfriars Playhouse indoor theater.

DID YOU KNOW?

A Cold Globe

The Icehotel in Sweden, which is built every autumn and melts every spring, has its own Globe Theatre most years. It was first built in 2003 and can seat 500 people. Actors perform in temperatures ranging from 17°F to –31°F (–8° to –35° C). Audiences are bundled up, and there are frequent intermissions so the actors and audiences can warm up!

A Shakespearian Indoor Theater for London

The United Kingdom has a reproduction indoor theater in Bristol, England. It was set up inside the Wickham Theatre of the University of Bristol so that students and academics could experiment with how such a theater would have been used. In 2014, Shakespeare's Globe opened a reproduction of an indoor theater, complete with candlelight. It also was built as much as possible using techniques and tools available at the time.

This is a virtual representation of the Sam Wanamaker Playhouse, the indoor theater at Shakespeare's Globe in London. It holds about 350 people, compared to about 1,500 in the Globe.

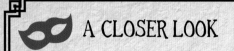
Shakespeare Festivals

Shakespeare festivals are held all around the world. Some have permanent theaters, while others set up a temporary theater each year. Some of the permanent theaters, such as the new Globe, Neuss, Germany, are reproductions of a Shakespearean theater. Most of these festivals run for just a few weeks at the same time each year, usually in the summer. Every state in the United States has at least one annual Shakespeare festival. In March 2010, the European Shakespeare Festivals Network was set up in Gdansk, Poland, to organize European festivals and publicize existing ones.

Individual Festivals

Some Shakespeare festivals have a permanent theater base and run for several months. They usually have their own acting company. The Shakespeare Theatre in Cedar City, Utah, runs from late June to mid-October. Other states have much smaller festivals that last just a week or so. There is a growing tradition of "Shakespeare in the Park"—entirely outdoor performances held in places such as public parks.

The Shakespeare Festival in Cedar City, Utah, leads off with a free outdoor show.

International Festivals

Some Shakespeare festivals are based in one country but invite companies from other countries to perform there. The Gdansk Shakespeare Festival, in Poland, began in 1993 as a Shakespeare Day. It grew into a weeklong festival with many companies from other countries performing. Other European festivals take place in Hungary, Armenia, the Czech Republic, and in Catalonia.

DID YOU KNOW?

The Neuss Globe

Since 1991, there has been a Shakespeare festival in the re-creation of Shakespeare's Globe on the racecourse at Neuss, in Germany. The 500-seat theater is open for a month and companies from all over the world give their versions of a Shakespeare play there. In 2012, Neuss had four companies from Germany; two each from France, Poland, and the United Kingdom; and one each from the United States and Kabul. It also had five other Shakespeare-related events, from lectures to other works inspired by Shakespeare.

A Changing World

The world of Shakespeare festivals is a changing one. Well-established festivals exist alongside new, smaller festivals that may, or may not, thrive and grow. But as the number of festivals that have been established continues to grow, we see that Shakespeare is as capable of getting enthusiastic interest today as he was 400 years ago.

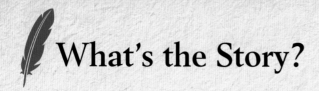

What's the Story?

In this book, we have looked at some of Shakespeare's plays in more detail than others. The following are summaries of the main plots of several of Shakespeare's most famous plays.

Macbeth

Macbeth is a loyal general to Duncan, King of Scotland. Three witches tell Macbeth he will become King of Scotland. Macbeth and his wife murder Duncan when he comes to stay at their castle. Duncan's sons flee Scotland. Macbeth becomes king, but also becomes suspicious of everyone around him. He kills those he suspects or, in the case of Macduff (who has left Scotland), their families. The witches convince Macbeth that he can't be beaten, but he is eventually killed by Macduff. Macduff defeats Macbeth's forces with an English army and puts Duncan's eldest son, Malcolm, on the throne.

Hamlet

The ghost of Hamlet's father tells Hamlet that his uncle, Claudius, murdered him to become king and marry Hamlet's mother. The ghost tells Hamlet to take revenge. Hamlet uses some traveling actors to test that Claudius is guilty, but afterward, he cannot bring himself to kill his uncle. He seems to go mad with his indecision and kills Polonius, the king's adviser, by mistake. Claudius sends Hamlet away, arranging to have him murdered. Hamlet returns and a bloodbath follows, at the end of which none of the main characters are alive.

A Midsummer Night's Dream

Hermia and Lysander want to marry. Hermia's father wants her to marry Demetrius. But Demetrius had originally wanted to marry Hermia's best friend, Helena, who still loves him. Hermia and Lysander run away to get married. Helena and Demetrius follow. In a wood outside Athens, the human world and the world of magic collide. Oberon the fairy king and his assistant, Puck, use a magic flower to confuse the lovers. Its juice, put in someone's eyes, makes them fall in love with the first thing they see on waking. The play ends happily with a triple wedding.

Romeo and Juliet

Romeo and Juliet fall in love, but their families are enemies. What can they do? They marry secretly, with the help of Juliet's nurse and a friar. Unfortunately, the family feud boils over into violence. Romeo kills Juliet's cousin and has to leave his home city of Verona, Italy. Juliet's parents try to force her to marry someone else. The friar comes up with a plan, but it ends in tragedy. For the lovers there can be no happy ending, although their deaths end the feud between the families.

King Lear

King Lear has three daughters. He decides to divide his kingdom between them. What they get depends on their telling him how much they love him. Goneril and Regan lie easily, exaggerating their love. The youngest, Cordelia, can't lie. Despite loving her father more, she gets nothing. Lear finds that without power his life is very different and that he, Goneril, and Regan make each other very unhappy. Lear goes mad. He is reunited with Cordelia, but it is too late. Cordelia dies, and Lear dies of grief.

Julius Caesar

Julius Caesar, a famous Roman general, is a popular Roman Consul—one of three consuls who led the Roman Republic. Many people fear that Caesar is going to make himself emperor and rule alone. A group of senators plot to kill Caesar, to stop him making himself emperor. Despite a warning, Caesar goes to the Senate and is killed. Rome falls apart and Caesar's adopted son (and nephew), Octavius, with the help of Mark Antony and other supporters, defeats his father's enemies and takes over Rome.

The Taming of the Shrew

Bianca wants to marry, but her sister, Katherina, is older and their father says Katherina has to marry first. No one wants to marry Katherina because of her terrible temper. Then Petruchio is persuaded to marry her. He treats her very badly. His excuse is that he is using falconry training tactics to tame her and make her happier. By the end of the play, Katherina has been "tamed," and she is an obedient wife.

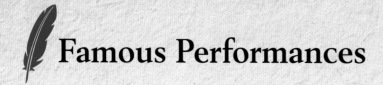

Famous Performances

There have been many famous performances of Shakespeare's plays. The ones below are just some of them. Some of these performances have been done both on stage and in movies. Watch some of the movies so you can see how acting styles have changed over the years!

Richard Burbage

Burbage was the actor who got all the main parts in the acting company that Shakespeare wrote for. He was very popular, and Shakespeare wrote many of his most famous roles for Burbage, including Richard III and King Lear.

David Garrick

Garrick was most famous for his performances in Shakespeare's tragedies, from 1741 on, especially as Richard III, Hamlet, and King Lear. He was famous because he performed more "naturally," getting into character and not just reciting the speeches.

Sarah Siddons

Siddons was especially famous for her performances as Lady Macbeth. When she performed it for the last time before giving up acting in 1812, the audience didn't let the play carry on after she had finished her last scene—they just stood and cheered.

Laurence Olivier in *Henry V*

Olivier played Henry V on stage and in a film made in 1944. World War II was being fought at the time. In the play, England defeats France in an important battle. The film lifted the spirits of the British people and encouraged them to continue fighting in World War II

Laurence Olivier in *Richard III*

Olivier played Richard III on stage several times from 1944 and in a film in 1955. His stage Richard III was so good that John Gielgud (another famous Shakespearean actor) gave him a very famous sword. The actor Edmund Kean had used the sword when he played Richard III. It was passed on to Henry Irving when he played Richard III, to praise his performance. Gielgud inherited the sword from his great-aunt, actress Ellen Terry (who inherited it from Irving). He then gave Olivier the sword as praise for his performance.

Paul Schofield in *King Lear*

In 1962, Peter Brook directed Paul Schofield in *King Lear*, having already directed him in a famous *Hamlet*. *King Lear* went on a world tour to packed audiences. Schofield's *King Lear* was also made into a movie in 1971. In 2004, the RSC asked a number of actors to vote for their greatest actor in a role and they chose Schofield's Lear.

Richard Burton in *Hamlet*

Burton was in the longest running *Hamlet* on Broadway in New York City. It was also made into a movie in 1964.

Richard Burton and Elizabeth Taylor in *The Taming of the Shrew*

Burton and Taylor made this movie in 1967. It was famous because they were married at the time and they were well known for fighting a lot, just like the characters in the play. It was also the first time Elizabeth Taylor performed in a Shakespeare play.

Peter Brook's production of *A Midsummer Night's Dream*

Brook produced the play for the RSC in 1970 and it is still referred to as "Brook's Dream." The performance was famous for several reasons. Brook used an empty white box for the set, few props, and dressed the cast in costumes from different times and places. He focused on the dangerous side of the fairies for the first time. The fairies' magic was shown as circus tricks. It started a trend for experimenting with how to perform the plays.

Antony Sher in *Richard III*

Sher played Richard III in 1984. The production was famous not only for being a very physical performance, but also for the amount of research that Sher did and documented in a book he wrote about playing the role: *The Year of the King*.

Mark Rylance as Olivia in *Twelfth Night*

Rylance played Olivia in *Twelfth Night* in 2002. It was an original practice performance that attracted large audiences. Many people had previously said that such a performance would not interest an average theater audience. It was performed in the same place (Middle Temple Hall, London) and on the same day (Twelfth Night, January 5) as Shakespeare's play—but 400 years later. A DVD of the play was released in 2012.

The Histories at Stratford

In 2008, the RSC put on the eight plays that are known as the Histories: *Richard II, Henry IV* (which is in two parts, each a play), *Henry V, Henry VI* (which is in three parts, each a play), and *Richard III*. Actors kept the same part over several plays for as long as the character was in the plays. They performed the Histories for two years, and even had a few "marathons" where they played them all over three days. Some "marathons" performed the plays in the order they were written. Others put on the plays with the rulers in chronological order. So on two days the audience saw three plays each day— morning, afternoon, and evening—with the remaining two plays on the third day.

Glossary

adaptation something changed from one format to another, such as a play to a film, or a short story to a musical

amateur someone who does something, such as performing plays, for enjoyment, not as a job or profession

British Empire all the lands outside Britain that the British took over and ruled

censorship suppression of anything considered morally or politically unacceptable

character a particular person in a play (such as the character of Juliet in *Romeo and Juliet*)

civil war war between different groups of people in the same country

classical to do with the cultures of the "classical age" of ancient Greece and ancient Rome

collaborate to work on something with another person

companies used here to mean groups of actors licensed by the same nobleman

contemporaries people who were alive at the same time

culture ideas, customs, and behavior of a particular group of people or time

dialogue conversation

director person who controls the production of a film or play. This involves choosing the actors, running rehearsals, and so on.

doublet name for a jacket with removable sleeves, popular in Shakespeare's time

essay short piece of writing on a factual subject

favor to favor a person or thing is to prefer it to other people or things

formal careful, following a set structure or rules

frames flat sides of a timber building

funding money given for a particular purpose

glover person who makes gloves, purses, and other similar things from leather

grammar school schools that were set up from the 14th century to teach young men. Subjects varied. Most schools taught the boys to read and write, in English and Latin. Many taught rhetoric. Some also taught Greek and other subjects, such as music.

iambic pentameter poetic verses with ten syllables to each line, split into five pairs. The second syllable of each pair is stressed.

imagery words used to give you a mental picture of something

indelicate rude or embarrassing

indoor theater theater that is part of a building, so not open to the sky

license official piece of paper that gives you permission to do something

manual used here to mean a book that explains how to do something

Master of the Revels in Shakespeare's time the person responsible for organizing the king or queen's entertainment and also reading plays and deciding what could be performed or saying what changes had to be made before performances could take place

mature student someone who becomes a student as an adult, rather than as a young person

national companies theater companies that see themselves as having a duty to provide theater for everyone in the country—both where the theater is based and on tour, as opposed to theaters that see themselves as serving the local community

nobleman from an important, wealthy, well-connected family

oratory art of speaking in public, including how to behave

original practices used here to mean a theater performance that only uses costumes, etc., available at the time the play was written

outdoor theater theater with a yard open to the sky, with roofed seating around a thrust stage with three sides

pitch to try to sell them an idea for a film, play, book, or invention

playwright someone who writes plays

prop movable objects used in a play, such as chairs, scrolls, plants, candlesticks, swords, and other items

prose writing without rhyme or metre

Puritan person who follows a strict Protestant religion

reconstruction the re-creation of something that no longer exists

rhetoric art of speaking in public, focusing on language

rub out slang for "kill"

scholar someone who is very knowledgeable about a particular subject

set in drama, the built-up scenery on a stage

setting where and when the action in the play takes place, such as ancient Greece or World War I

sonnet 14-line poem with 10 syllables to each line

sophisticated experienced and worldly-wise

Soviet to do with the Soviet Union (USSR). This country broke up into many others, including Russia, in late 1991.

tailor someone who makes clothes

take a view or idea about something

theater companies groups of actors who work together all the time, either in a particular theater or on tour

thrust stage stage that sticks out so the audience surrounds it on three sides

tone sound of something, such as deep, high, soft, or loud

tour actors are on tour when they perform the show in different places around the country

verse poetry that rhymes

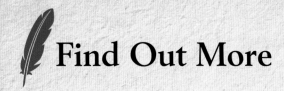

Find Out More

Books

Foster, Brett. *Shakespeare's Life.* New York: Chelsea House, 2012.

Robson, David. *Shakespeare's Globe Theater.* San Diego, CA: Reference Point Press, 2013.

Web Sites

www.shakespeare.org.uk/explore-shakespeare/about-shakespeare.html
Find out more about William Shakespeare on this web site.

www.touchpress.com/titles/shakespeares-sonnets
The language of Shakespeare's sonnets can seem complicated. But each one hangs on a single idea that is given to you in the first few lines. Try sonnets 18 and 138. You can hear them read out on this web site.

www.mckellen.com/writings/8204shakesq.htm
This site has an interview about a one-man show featuring actor Ian McKellen.

Places to Visit

Where you can visit depends on where you live and what you can afford, but here are a few suggestions:

- a local reproduction theater (see the map on page 45)
- a professional Shakespeare production. Think about where and when the director has chosen to set the production and how that affects your reaction to it.
- an amateur Shakespeare production. Some are very good, and Shakespeare plays were meant to be performed, not read.

Suggestions for Further Research

Here are a few suggestions for research, to develop ideas raised in this book:

- Find out more about a Shakespeare festival. You could choose one close to where you live, or one in a different part of the world entirely. Discover how long it runs for and the companies that perform. Does it have a permanent performance space, does it put up a temporary building each year, or is it open-air?

Index

acting companies 5, 10, 44
adaptations and borrowings 22–33, 37
all-female productions 20
amended plays 29
authorship debate 6–7

Bacon, Francis 6
Bailey, Lucy 11
bardolatry 41
Beatles 19
Blunt, Emily 14
borrowings by Shakespeare 34–37
bowdlerization 29
Boyd, Michael 26
Brook, Peter 59, 60
Burbage, Richard 30, 38, 58
Burton, Richard 20, 59

censorship 12
collaborative writing 7
comic scenes 14, 15
copyright 5
costumes 9, 10, 12, 13

DiCaprio, Leonardo 16
directors 11–13, 16, 18

Elizabeth I 7

festivals 10, 26, 40, 41, 46, 54–55
film and TV 16–19, 20, 21, 22, 25, 27, 37
First Folio 5
Forrest, Edwin 42

Garrick, David 28, 29, 39, 40, 41, 58
Globe theater 8, 10, 11, 27, 39, 41, 48–51
graphic novels 4
groundlings 50
Gwyn, Nell 38

Hamlet 9, 11, 16, 18, 20–21, 23, 25, 27, 31, 32–33, 56, 58, 59
Henry V 16, 58

hip-hop 23
Histories 60

iambic pentameter 30
indoor theaters 39, 46–47, 52, 53
influence of Shakespeare 4–5, 22–33, 40–41

James I 36, 37
jigs 8
Jonson, Ben 7
Julius Caesar 11, 12, 13, 43, 57

King Lear 26, 29, 35, 57, 58, 59
Kurosawa, Akira 26

language, English 5, 30–31
life of Shakespeare 6
Luhrmann, Baz 16

Macbeth 4, 11, 15, 16, 22, 24, 26, 28, 36–37, 39, 42, 56, 58
McKellen, Ian 16, 17
Macready, William 42
Marlowe, Christopher 7, 34
Master of the Revels 12
A Midsummer Night's Dream 13, 19, 22, 24, 27, 35, 56, 60
Moore, Christopher 6
Much Ado About Nothing 22, 23, 35, 51
music 8
musicals 24

Noh theater 9

Olivier, Laurence 16, 20, 58–59
operas 24, 29
Ophelia 32–33
oratory 9
original practices 8–9, 60
Othello 18, 23, 24
outdoor theaters 10, 39, 46, 47, 52
Oxford, Earl of 7

performance 8–21

performances, famous 58–60
plots 34, 35
poetry 30, 40
political messages 12, 13
props 8

reactions to Shakespeare 42–43
reading Shakespeare 14
recognizable personalities 14
reconstructed theaters 8, 44, 45, 46–53
Reduced Shakespeare Company 23
rhetoric 9
Richard III 16, 17, 39, 40, 58, 59, 60
Romeo and Juliet 13, 14, 16, 24, 29, 34, 35, 57
Royal Shakespeare Company (RSC) 4, 11, 13, 26, 28, 47, 59, 60
Rylance, Mark 60

Schofield, Paul 59
settings 12, 13
Sher, Antony 60
Siddons, Sarah 58
special effects 8
Stewart, Patrick 37
Stratford-upon-Avon 4, 6, 40

The Taming of the Shrew 11, 18, 22, 25, 57, 59
Taylor, Elizabeth 18, 59
The Tempest 22, 24, 35, 39
Tennant, David 20, 21
theater closures 39
thrust stage 15, 19, 46, 47
ticket prices 16
timeless themes 14
Titus Adronicus 11, 23, 27
translations 26–27
Twelfth Night 8, 35, 60

Venkatrathnam, Sonny 42–43

Wanamaker, Sam 48
West Side Story 24